My State TEXAS

By Christina Earley

TABLE OF CONTENTS

A Crabtree Seedlings Book

Crabtree Publishing
crabtreebooks.com

School-to-Home Support for Caregivers and Teachers

This book helps children grow by letting them practice reading. Here are a few guiding questions to help the reader build his or her comprehension skills. Possible answers appear in red.

Before Reading:

- What do I know about Texas?
    - *I know that Texas is a state.*
    - *I know that Texas has beaches.*

- What do I want to learn about Texas?
    - *I want to learn which famous people were born in Texas.*
    - *I want to learn what the state flag looks like.*

During Reading:

- What have I learned so far?
    - *I have learned that Austin is the state capital of Texas.*
    - *I have learned that there are many reptiles in the Guadalupe Mountains.*

- I wonder why...
    - *I wonder why the state flower is the bluebonnet.*
    - *I wonder why there are caverns near San Antonio.*

After Reading:

- What did I learn about Texas?
    - *I have learned that Johnson Space Center has rockets you can see up close.*
    - *I have learned that the state animal is the Texas longhorn.*

- Read the book again and look for the glossary words.
    - *I see the word **capital** on page 6, and the word **icon** on page 18. The other glossary words are found on pages 22 and 23.*

TEXAS
Hi! My name is Santiago.
Welcome to Texas!

I live in San Antonio. I like to ride in a **river taxi** along the River Walk.

San Antonio is the most visited city in Texas.

Texas is in the south-central United States. The **capital** is Austin.

Fun Fact: Houston is the largest city in Texas.

The state animal is the Texas **longhorn**.

The bluebonnet is
the state flower.

We grow a lot of cotton. Most of it is used to make clothes.

Fun Fact: More than 35% of cotton in the U.S. is grown in Texas.

My state flag has a star. Texas is called the "Lone Star State."

There are 11 national sports teams in Texas.

I like to visit Guadalupe Mountains National Park. There are many kinds of animals to see.

Fun Fact: More than 50 kinds of reptiles live in the Guadalupe Mountains.

I can see rockets up close at Johnson Space Center.

I have fun with my family at the beaches of Galveston Island.

Music **icon** Beyoncé was born in Texas. NFL **quarterback** Patrick Mahomes was also born in Texas.

Fun Fact: President Dwight D. Eisenhower was born in Denison, Texas.

I love traveling to different **caverns** near San Antonio.

I enjoy backpacking in Big Bend National Park.

Glossary

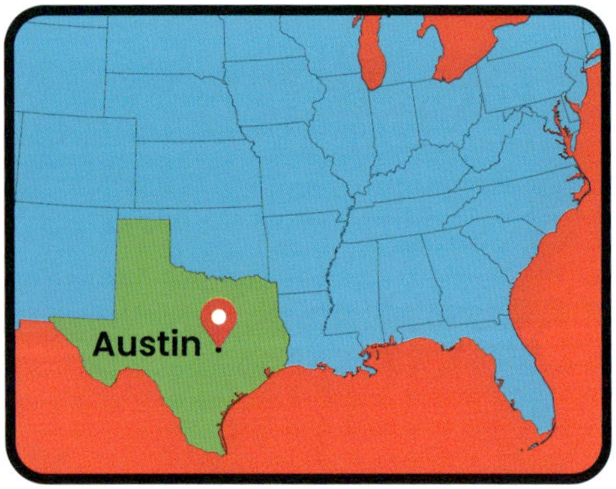

capital (cap-ih-tuhl): The city or town where the government of a country, state, or province is located

caverns (kav-ernz): Large caves, usually underground

icon (i-kon): A very famous person

longhorn (long-horn): A type of cattle with long horns

quarterback (kwor-ter-bak): A position on a football team

river taxi (riv-er tax-ee): A boat that takes people from place to place

Index

About the Author

Christina Earley lives in sunny South Florida with her husband and son. She enjoys traveling around the United States and learning about different historical places. Her hobbies include hiking, yoga, and baking.

Written by: Christina Earley

Designed and Illustrated by: Bobbie Houser

Series Development: James Earley

Proofreader: Melissa Boyce

Educational Consultant: Marie Lemke M.Ed.

Photographs:
Alamy: GL Archive: p. 19
Newscom: Scott Winters/Icon Sportswire DGM: p. 18 right, 23
Shutterstock: Joe Belanger: cover; Sean Pavone: p. 3, 5; f11photo: p. 4, 23; Volina: p. 6, 22; travelview: p. 7; Quinn Calder: p. 8, 23; Leena Robinson: p. 9; Trong Nguyen: p. 10-11; Natalia Bratslavsky: p. 11; David Lee: p. 12; Keeton Gale: p. 13; Invisible Witness: p. 14-15; Danita Delimont: p. 15; John_Silver: p. 16; Mark Taylor Cunningham: p. 17; Tinseltown: p. 18 left, 22; John Le: p. 20, 22; Zack Frank: p. 21

Crabtree Publishing

crabtreebooks.com 800-387-7650

Printed in the U.S.A./012023/CG20220815

Published in Canada
Crabtree Publishing
616 Welland Avenue
St. Catharines, Ontario
L2M 5V6

Published in the United States
Crabtree Publishing
347 Fifth Avenue
Suite 1402-145
New York, New York, 10016

Library and Archives Canada Cataloguing in Publication
Available at Library and Archives Canada

Library of Congress Cataloging-in-Publication Data
Available at the Library of Congress

Hardcover: 978-1-0396-9655-6
Paperback: 978-1-0396-9762-1
Ebook (pdf): 978-1-0396-9976-2
Epub: 978-1-0396-9869-7